DR BASHABI FRASER, CBE, Hon[...] dren's writer, editor and acade[...] Woman of Scotland by the Sa[...] Bashabi has authored and [...] creative articles and been widely [...] publications include *Patient Dignity* (2021) and *Kavir[...]* [...]re (2019). She is the Chief Editor of the international, peer-reviewed e-journal *Gitanjali and Beyond*, and sits on the Editorial Board of *WritersMosaic*.

Bashabi is Professor Emerita of English and Creative Writing at Edinburgh Napier University and Director of the Scottish Centre of Tagore Studies (SCOTS). She is also an Honorary Fellow at the Centre for South Asian Studies, University of Edinburgh, Honorary Vice President of the Association of Scottish Literary Studies (ASLS) and a Royal Literary Fund Fellow.

Praise for *Habitat*

Bashabi Fraser's timely new collection, *Habitat*, speaks with an acute awareness of the richness of our world and of the perils that increasingly confront it. A great gallery of birds, trees, cats and people, in landscapes of her two countries, India and Scotland, are vividly present here in poems of many shapes, all full of a love that is both fearful and full of hope.—PETER FRANCE

A warm and passionate hymn to the richness of the planet, from the Arctic to Arthur's Seat, Glasgow to Kolkata, lamenting the losses of nature in our time but exulting in human relationships, journeys and 'the call of home'.—RUTH PADEL

I headed straight for the birds – well, that was the idea, but I got waylaid by the Prologue and the Foreword, particularly those fireflies dancing to a subtle rhythm and rhyme scheme, scattering 'our suppressed thoughts'. So I left the river to its 'churning burial ground of eternal oblivion' only to find that the first bird to speak is caged and full of righteous anger, and then that it submits its freedom to serve a caged human. These poems come tumbling out of a copious basket. Observation is sharp and there is much humanity and positivity. They speak straight to you. That's why I like them so much.—JOHN PURSER

In these dark days for the planet, what shines through Bashabi's work is a deep love for family and friends, for humanity at large and the natural world. Spiritual at their core, the poems celebrate our oneness, sing their song of hope.—ALAN SPENCE

One of the effects of the climate crisis has been the vitality of a poetry that is decidedly public-facing; a poetry whose urgency often dispenses with the page. The tensions behind such a development run through *Habitat*. The core of the collection may be found in personal encounters, but its 'argument' extends far beyond that. The 'habitat' – the community of which Bashabi Fraser writes – encompasses all living things. It is a book rich in praise, but also freighted with warning.—TOM POW

COVER IMAGE

'Everlastingly' by Vibha Pankaj, oil on canvas, was inspired by the artist's memories of the abode provided by the banyan tree mingled with Scottish oak and juniper. The Firth of Forth in the background is unquestionably Edinburgh.
www.vibhaartist.com; #vibha_artist

By the Same Author:

Poetry
Life, collected poems, Edinburgh: Diehard Publishers, 1997
Edinburgh: An Intimate City, an illustrated anthology of contemporary poetry on Edinburgh, co-edited with Elaine Greig. Edinburgh: The City of Edinburgh Council, 2000
With Best Wishes from Edinburgh, Indian edition of collected poems, Introduction by Debjani Chatterjee. Kolkata: Writers Workshop, 2001
Rainbow World, Poems from many cultures, edited with Debjani Chatterjee. London: Hodder, 2003
Tartan & Turban, Edinburgh: Luath Press, 2004
From the Ganga to the Tay, Edinburgh: Luath Press, 2009
Ragas and Reels, with photographs by Hermann Rodrigues. Edinburgh: Luath Press, 2012
Scots Beneath the Banyan Tree: Stories from Bengal, Edinburgh: Luath Press, 2012
Letters to My Mother and Other Mothers, Edinburgh: Luath Press, 2015
The Homing Bird. Devon: Indigo Dreams Publishing, 2017
Thaali Katori: An Anthology of Scottish South Asian Poetry, Co-editor with Alan Riach. Edinburgh: Luath Press, 2017
My Mum's Sari, illustrated by Zoe Barnish. London: BBC Word Wave Bitesize Series, 2019 Also in an audio recording, available at bbc.co.uk/bitesize/topics/z74n6v4/articles/zfwdkmn
Patient Dignity, Edinburgh: Scotland Street Press, 2021

Plays
The Ramayana, a stage and a screen play (commissioned by Scottish Arts Council with Edinburgh Puppet Lab). Jaipur: Aadi Publishers, 2019

Non-fiction
A Meeting of Two Minds: The Geddes Tagore Letters, edited and introduced. Edinburgh: Wordpower, 3rd edition, revised, 2005
Bengal Partition Stories: An Unclosed Chapter, edited and introduced. London, Anthem Press, revised edition, 2006
Rabindranath Tagore's Global Vision, guest edited issue of *Literature Compass*, Vol 12, Issue 5, May 2015
A Confluence of Minds: The Rabindranath Tagore and Patrick Geddes Reader on Education and Environment, Co-editor with Tapati Mukherjee and Amrit Sen. Shantiniketan: Visva-Bharati Press; Edinburgh: Luath Press, 2017

Scottish Orientalism and the Bengal Renaissance: The Continuum of Ideas, co-editor with Tapati Mukherjee and Amrit Sen. Shantiniketan: Visva-Bharati Press; Edinburgh: Luath Press, 2017
Rabindranath Tagore, London: Reaktion Books; Chicago University Press, Critical Lives Series, 2019
Lakshmi's Footprints and Paisley Patterns: The Scoto-Indian Interface, edited by Bashabi Fraser and Debnarayan Bandyopadhyay. London and New York: Routledge, 2023

Children's fiction
Topsy Turvy, Calcutta: Dasgupta & Co. Pvt. Ltd., 2004
Just One Diwali Night, Calcutta: Dasgupta & Co. Pvt. Ltd., 2004

Habitat

BASHABI FRASER

Luath Press Limited
EDINBURGH
www.luath.co.uk

Dedication

David Attenborough for raising awareness and instilling love in us
for the richness of our planet

Greta Thunberg for her defence of it

and my father, Bimalendu Bhattacharya, for his powerful books on
a sustainable future

Some of these poems have appeared in *PENnings*, *Paint the Sky with Stars* (2005), *Hidden City* (2006), *Letters to My Mother and Other Mothers* (2015), *Bengal Lights* (2014), *The Mighty Stream: Poems in Celebration of Martin Luther King* (2017), Goutam Karmakar, ed., *The Lie of the Land* (2019) and *SETU* (2019).

First published 2023

ISBN: 978-1-80425-093-8

The author's right to be identified as author of this book
under the Copyright, Designs and Patents Act 1988 has been asserted.

The paper used in this book is recyclable. It is made from low-chlorine pulps produced in a low-energy, low-emission manner from renewable forests and other controlled sources.

Printed and bound by
Hobbs the Printers Ltd., Totton

Typeset in 11 point Sabon LT by
Main Point Books, Edinburgh

© Bashabi Fraser 2023

Contents

Introduction by Joyce Caplan   11

PROLOGUE
The White Page   15
Earthrise   17
Fireflies   18
A Lonely Race   20
Deforestation   21
As the Ice Melts   23
When Disaster Threatens   24
Wind and Gorse: On Arthur's Seat   25
Let us Ring in the Change   26

BIRDSPEAK
Freedom's Call   31
The Free Bird Wills   32
The Guest: In a House in North Kolkata   34
Kolkata: From Nabanna's 9th Floor   37
Our Bird Table   38
The Robin's Complaint   41
Come Robin, Come   42
In My Nest   43
The Curlew's Egg   44
The Racing Pigeon   45
Seagulls   46
Sonnet from a Crow   47

Monarch of the Bazaar	48
The Crow	50
The Sprightly Sparrow	52
Darkling I Listen	54
The Eagle's Epic Journey	56
The Rock Climber's Vision	57
The Osprey's Observation	58
Crepuscular: The Urbanised Prowler	60
Night Watchers	62
Serenading a Peahen	63
The Monsoons Break	65
I am Not Your National Bird Here	66
A Blackbird	69
A Heron Sanctuary	70
The Meeting Point: Mohona	72
The Glasgow Thief	74
Homecoming: In Search of Petrol in Loch Lomond Country	75
A Valued Sentry: In Aberdeen	76
In Holyrood Park	78
At Hampstead Heath	79
Pages from the Memoirs of a Battery Hen	81
What the Birds Say	84
The Owl and the Elephant	85
A Heavenly Concourse: In a Shattered Land	86
A Time to Leave	87

CATTERY: A CAT TRILOGY

Mishti: Our Black Cat	91
Toffee: Our Ginger Cat	92
Noah: Our Felix Cat	94
The Unreachable Dream	96

THE DISTANT AND THE NEAR

In Tiger Country	99
Inseparable: Wild Things	101
Born to Be Free	102
The Hungry Ocean	105
The Storm	106
The Sea which Sustains, Kills	107
Let Me Be	109
The Dry Season Ends	110
The Bypassing Monsoons in June: From Kolkata	111
Everest	112
On the Shore	113
Seals and Shags at Plockton Firth	114
The Rare Red Fox	115
Anxiety in the Glen	116
The Galloping Vision: In Inverness-shire	117
Migration	119
Missives of Music	122
The Distant and the Near	123

EPILOGUE

A Message	127

Introduction

THESE POEMS ARE about writing itself, from the Prologue to the Epilogue. How we fill 'the white space' with words that describe and recreate the worlds around us – our habitat.

They challenge form and perception by abandoning punctuation, to free meaning and us to a myriad of interpretations. In this strange post-pandemic time it reminds us that all our normal markers have been erased. Yet the poems are also embedded firmly in place and our response to it,

> Fluttering like a hundred doves in flight
> Wanting to alight with the call of home

The world of nature in these poems continues thriving and adapting: birds, cats, forest animals, the sea, the winds, all survive despite our greed and exploitation that destroy many habitats including our own with indifference.

Bashabi has lived in two countries and this duality informs her writing with both parallels and divergence. We have peacocks in Scotland and India. Descriptions of urban chaos and rural struggle.

Birds wing their way through many poems as symbols of transcendence and release. We are taken into their spaces with intense observation and empathy.

Cats also inhabit complex environments as they negotiate relationships with the human owners who are reciprocally 'enslaved by your alertness and stupidity'.

We interact with nature by projecting onto it our own expectations and disappointments, our own desires and fears. It makes us look at ourselves, as these poems do, as both intruders and facilitators.

Water is another medium of chaos that has both containment and change, for it both destroys and sustains us.

> Let me ride the surging crest
> Let me see a confluence
> That gives sustenance
>
> Where you and I can wander free
> Create and live with dignity

There are many poems dedicated to friends and colleagues to emphasise that we are part of the world of humanity, and not apart from it. These poems are delightfully fitted to the personalities of the dedicatees and to their concerns and place in the wider community.

In this collection we make many journeys, enriched by Bashabi's own experience but made to reflect on our own as inhabitants of a shared habitat. May 'our gardens be warm with hope'.

Joyce Caplan

PROLOGUE

The White Page
To Neil

*The forest calls out
from its still centre
to the leaf of the book
that came from its heart
in the silent scream
of a shared creative agony.*

The white space
Is like a still lake
Undiscovered in
An emerald grove,
Its silence borne
From the depths
Of a forest
From which
It was torn –
The screams
Of death
Unuttered
But smothered
In our factories
And gathered
Into pages
Waiting to be
Ruffled into
Ripples that will
Shatter the surface
And reveal
The secret
Of sighs

Of rustling leaves,
The shooting
Desires of tendrils
The wisdom
Of the dark bark
And ambition
Of branches
Waiting to find
A voice to spill
Over and fill
The white space.

Earthrise
To Baba

The earth in incandescent light
Its swirling surface emblematic of life
Tilts to capture what is its right
From its incessant source of energy.

The image of this resplendent dawn
Was imprinted on our consciousness
Its startling beauty has lived on
Against the cold geology

Of her satellite's stark horizon
Round whom we wove our fantasies
A madness we can now with reason
Rise above, to cherish this prodigy

This planet earth which is sending us a message for revival
As urgent as our will to prosper and our ultimate survival.

Fireflies

The veil of darkness descends
Draping fields and forest
In obscurity

The silence of those who might
Have spoken hovers like a brooding
Cloud with intensity.

As lost travellers, we stumble through
Undergrowth, wishing for the moon
To emerge.

When sparklers of delight startle
Our footsteps, flitting with frolic
From branch and hedge,

They twinkle and challenge the
Cold distant starlight as they
Sing of the earth –

They hum in harmony, trapezing with joy
They trip with the rhythm of ripples
Of mirth

They glow with the magic of a dreamland
They cascade with the cadence of a fountain
In spring

They dispel the gloom of low, looming clouds
Their fairy lights festoon the darkness
With wings

They whisper, they beckon, they urge
Us to join their dance of true freedom
From fear

They lift up our spirits with sparkle and glitter
They scatter our suppressed thoughts and stall
Our tears.

A Lonely Race

A river's journey is long and lonely
Like the veteran long distance runner
A challenge from start to finish
An adventure at every ripple of my flow.
I have no consort or companion
No mother's arms, no sibling's rivalry –
I am a witness through time
I revel in reminiscence and reflection
I mirror heaven's fury and kindness
I salute panoramic vistas
I lash past every urban sprawl
And lap round humble villages.

I am a solitary meanderer
Journeying to my finishing line
Which does not make me a champion
But swallows my singular identity
In a churning burial ground of eternal oblivion.

Deforestation
To Mandy Haggith

When you walk beneath my boughs
They make a canopy above your gaze –
So intricate that the sky appears in glimpses
And if you invade my domain
You will find your steps impeded by the foliage
That flourishes between the stalwart trunks
Of my populace – this earth's rich heritage.

You can feel the deep silence of my presence
Which embraces your every alert sense.

This is where the leopards lurk
The deer stand still or leap away,
Here I have the fox's den
The pheasant's call, the rhino's horn
The bison herds between my bark
And birds of every hue and cry
Send sharp signals
To all prey
Who slink away
Amidst my intense density
Where monkeys chatter
And squirrels scatter
Nuts and fruits
Against my roots
And blooms that vie
In shape and colour
To attract and capture
The insect life that is enraptured
By the habitat I provide.

But you have set a tidal wave
That sweeps under the forest glade
Pushing my treeline back
To the edge of life's brink.
You have cleared me to plant cash crops
You have cleared me to graze cattle
You have cleared me to cultivate
You have cleared me to build your homes,
Your roads, your factories and fires,
To paper walls, to write your tales,
To feed your staggering race
That overfills this planet's face.

You have set in motion soil erosion
You have let mudslides crush.
My roots that keep the earth soil porous,
Now removed, cause floods that flash.

Every day you calmly clear
Vast swathes of virgin forests that stand
Between you and your destruction.
So twelve million hectares
Disappear every year.

This is a war you now wage
With cutting-edge technology –
Bulldozers that neatly raze
And road graders and log skidders
That bare the earth's surface –
Till in a hundred years from now
My forests will exist no more
Replaced by a silence
More terrifying than war.

As the Ice Melts
To Baba

As the ice melts in the Arctic zone
Himalayan peaks are not alone
Having their silence disturbed
By frequent avalanches hurled
Into the icy seas. The sea level rises steadily
Crashing down craggy slopes to cause
Flash floods that readily
Destroy life on widening plains
Where rivers swell from lightening rains
And as glaciers shrink through time
Upsetting rivers in their prime
The sea colonises the land
And rivers break their natural bond
Towns and crops are surprised
When submerged or deprived
As each year we release new fumes
Of eight billion tons over our homes
In heat-trapped carbon dioxide
And methane that now provides
An encasing warmth that chokes this earth
This swirling mass that gave us birth.

When Disaster Threatens

When the frost lies laced and hoary,
                         hardening ground and grass
I will breathe upon its hardness
                         and melt its surface glass
When the clouds spread grey and thick,
                         curtaining sun and sky
I will gather their grim curtain
                         and wring it gently dry
When the sea rises to battle
                         with the unresisting land
I'll quell its warring cry
                         with the pressure of my hand
And when the peoples of the world
                         are ready to destroy
I'll tell the sun to leave its sphere
                         to prevent another Troy.

Wind and Gorse: On Arthur's Seat
To the bhajis on the hills – my walking friends' group

The wind was the enemy
An aggressive bully
Who schemed to hurl
Us off the slope. Even the slippery
Ground and unanchored rocks
Were willing to stay supine,
Refraining from tripping us
Off our balance as we
Aimed for the final peak.

The warmth was in the gorse
Its sunny mustard plenitude
Caressing the eye, hugging the slopes
Burnished by Apollo, the
Colour of love, of kisses,
Promises and erotica
Blazing on Arthur's Seat, daring
The sullen wind to tear it apart –
Resistant, resplendent and radiant.

Let us Ring in the Change

For Jim Stewart

Let us work our white magic
To roll back the ocean
And whisper to islands
That don't see the sun
Let us bid them to rise
And unfold their green mantle,
Rustle with life
And greet the horizon.

Let us tingle the heart strings
Of sarod and esraj[1]
To charm back the forests
That we slashed down and burnt
Let us silence the dark dirge
Of desert and shorn hills
And fill them with music
Of willow and birch.

---

[1] An Indian classical string instrument.

Let us dance with the peacocks
To beckon the storm clouds
To swell every stream
And ripple the lakes
Let us push back the concrete
And lift the smog curtain
To send out a message for the
Wild wind to awake.

Let us bring back a smile
To the wan moon above
Who will know that her
Beloved planet will live.

BIRDSPEAK

Freedom's Call

For Martin Luther King Jr

You met me in my day of success
When I sang to celebrate my freedom
Of flight across a boundless sky

I was at the treetop height of bliss
When you captured me from my skydom
Chained me and forbid me to fly.

Today I sit in your dull steel cage
My wings are static by my side
I survive on fragments you throw here

My endless joy has turned to rage
My urge to fly does not subside
I feel a surging wave of fear

Sweep through my frozen little frame
It flows with intent through this lair
It shoots like arrows through these bars

It startles you like summer rain
A song that challenges and dares
The rising wind and the distant star.

So I will sing to freedom's call
I will dream of trees ablaze
With colours that the molten sun

Has decreed for one and all.

The Free Bird Wills
For Rabindranath Tagore

I saw your upturned face
As you marked my ascent
Riding the rising wind,
Then splintering the sunbeams
In my decided descent.
You heard my song before
You saw me, my unfettered
Joy, which rolled back
The horizon, soothed the far
Seas and left the stars scattered
Beyond the Milky Way.
I knew you were not free
To leave, to step out, to let
The breeze lift your anchal,[1]
To feel the sun tingle your
Bangled arms, and let
The music of the stars witness
Your dreaming escapades that
Can never lead you astray.

---

[1] The end of the sari that is slung over the left shoulder.

I flew in on a whim
In your untold dreams,
I entered your gilded cage
Where I will tarry and age –
Your captive, held by you.

I will watch the morning dew
Fall with you, I will stir the sun
Across the rainbow arch from dawn
Till dusk. I will wear your silver chain,
I will sing for you again,
I have come to share your walls
Willingly, where my colours enthral
Your dull whitewashed days.

The Guest: In a House in North Kolkata
To Kumkum, Babuni and Nupur

This wayward wind that
Whizzes past motley
Buildings of diverse heights,
Tearing through winding streets
That jostle between
Time's fragmented memories,
Tells me that the Ganga
Flows somewhere close by
Sending this missive
Of its reviving reality.

This is the wind I miss
As I travel further south
To a part of the city
Where Ganga seems a myth.

But as I stand here
On this narrow balcony
Which cradles this house
Like a comforting arm,
I am surprised by a gift
Borne by this wind
In a yellow budgerigar,
Bright as new corn,
The kiss of the golden sun
On its feathers, who chooses
My balustrade to rest
From its stormy ride.

Where have you come
From my little bird
Bearing a missive from
Ganga's whispering breast?
Why do you let me
Speak to you and why
Do you hop willingly
Onto my outstretched arm,
A consenting prisoner
Or a gracious guest
Choosing my proffered cage
As your place of rest?

And you stay with me,
Happy to flit around
Your bounded world
While the wind capers free.
Is it because you are
Tired of being whisked
Like the palash[1] blossoms
And the mango manjari[2]
By a wanton wind
Released from Ganga's
Breast? Here we will
Sing together, content
With the certainty
Of regular meals
And rest. Not threatened

---

[1] A deciduous tree with flaming orange blossoms common to North India, blooming from January to March. Its botanical name is *Butea Monosperma*. The Battle of Plassey in 1757, which the British won in India against Siraj ud-Daulah, Nawab of Bengal, was probably fought at a place with Palash trees, called Palashi, mispronounced/misspelt in British history as Plassey.
[2] A collection of flowers – so here, the mango blossoms.

By the heady ride
Of a thoughtless wind
That rules the tide
As the Ganga flows
Wide to greet the
Bay where the sky
Stoops down and storms begin.

Kolkata: From Nabanna's 9th floor[1]
To Neeta Das, Ishita Majumdar and Charles Bruce

These are my Brooklyn Heights
The ambitious city's fugitive flight
To escape the tired, tedious streets
And seek the peace of cloud retreats.

From here the coils of arteries
Of flyovers, bridges, lines of trees
Are necklaced, festooned festively
In measured strokes of artistry.

The river ruminates below
A distant, sluggish, dreamy flow
The sun slopes down, the grey haze clears
The marvellous Howrah Bridge appears.

When from the depths of heaven's way
A regal kite salutes the day
Its powerful wings hold back the wind
It glides and views us trapped within

A glass which frames this skyhover
A mighty monarch and rover
Free to glide and free to roam
Free to ride the gust and gloam

And scrutinise each narrow road
And read the city's every mood
A witness in whose memory
Is held this city's history.

---
[1] Nabanna is a new building where the West Bengal State Government has its offices.

Our Bird Table
To Alison Fraser

Our bird table stands behind
The French windows of our kitchen
From where we can watch without
Causing feathery flutter and flight
As birds fly across and alight
Under the sloping roof of this shelter
On a tripod, the perfect camera
To record a motion picture of flurries
From the tall hedge and back, as they
Feed, fetch and carry, whisk away
In a hurry, with the twitch of a tail
– For any time is meal time –
And more so if the sun shines.

The dunnocks come in pairs
Playing out a two times table
From the old world number book
In twos and fours, and eights and tens
From one February to another
November – so like sparrows
Apart from the jerky bob that
Gives away their identity, enough
For us to forget the sorrow of losing
A once familiar breed.

Then there are the families of
Blackbirds, who balance their
Quail feather pen tails at sharp
Angles away from the tray.

The pigeons come in solo shows,
Plump and full-blown, each sits
On the roof to contemplate
The tray below, wondering
How best to turn sideways and
Bend to catch the crumbs at
The end of each meditative
Session. Between the pigeons
And the doves, the birdseed
And bread are tapped up
With nodding speed, keeping
The tray above and the patio
Beneath clean as the ground
After a shower. They don't
Know how to stop till the last
Grain is gobbled and stored
Away, so they can
Hobble away and wait till
The next day for scattered grains
Which draw the sharp eye
Of the magpie, looking for gains
On the paving stones;
Though sometimes it will undergo
The self-inflicted torture
Of sitting on the sloping structure
And twisting precariously to earn
A spot of breakfast from below
Where its tail gets in the way
Like a flamenco dancer's trail.

And in between the larger guests
Come the playful gypsies
Of blue-tits, finches and linnets
And the stalwart robin
Bobbing in and out
But never deserting us
Even when the peak season wanes
As the long daylight hours
Are squeezed out and flowers fade
Our bird-table stands as an
Invitation for free flights for the redbreast
In the bleak months of winter shade.

The Robin's Complaint
To Debjani Chatterjee and Brian D'Arcy

You don't have a barn anymore
But a shed with a tightly shut door
There isn't any hay
Where I can snugly stay
So I live by your evergreen hedge
Tucked under your window ledge
But I do like the nuts
                  strung from the tree
That you leave out in winter
                  for my mate and me.

Come Robin, Come

Come Robin, come
For the pale winter sun
Cannot keep you warm.

Stay Robin, stay
In my garden today
And don't fly away.

Sing Robin, sing
Through winter mornings
Till the coming of spring.

Eat Robin, eat
The crumbs at your feet
Before you retreat.

Go Robin, go
Before the white snow
Fills the hedgerow.

Rest Robin, rest
My little redbreast
Curled in your nest.

In My Nest

I have searched far and wide
And picked my gems with pride
In feathers light and swift
In cotton – white and soft
I have lined my walls with care
Where no sharp eagles dare
To soar

And when the sky is tender
With the spring sun's splendour
When the new-born leaves unfurl
When a fresh breeze stirs the world
You can greet life in the east
And I will welcome you to rest
In my safe and gracious nest
And grow.

The Curlew's Egg
To Stephen Regan

The fields had the feel of the soft
Damp feathers of a pigeon's back
Smoothed by stroking fingers
Nestling in my palm, spent and slack.
Amidst the farmer's scooped out furrows
Led by the alluring light of the setting sun
I found this egg, large enough to fill the hollow
Of my hand, cold and abandoned by a curlew
Destined to be the star collection
Of my sawdust trophies – a lion king
Brushed beautifully by the light brown tales
Under dark brown splotches, awaiting unravelling.

The Racing Pigeon
To Stephen Regan

I could see it reel in an uncertain wheel
As it curbed its trail and came to rest
In the nest it shared with my lot
For seven nights. It ate out of my hand
Its ring tickling my small hand, eyeing me
With caution. It proved a tumbler all right –
One sharply defined morning, when its time came
It put on the best acrobatic show, somersaulting
In neat circles, before it raced home.

Seagulls
To Shanu

Ubiquitous presence
Gleaming, glistening white
Reflecting the purity of daylight
The watchful essence
Of the seafarer's vigil
Intensely intent and still.

This city listens pensively
To your call, startlingly raucous,
Forestalling debate, gratingly coarse –
Yet there you are, pervasively
Swooping from your gliding watch
To seek each lamp post for your urban perch.

In the unhappening hour at noon
Your cries evoke nostalgic dreams
Your seeking voice chasing lost streams –
As you find strength in numbers, festooned
On rooftops of terraced retreats
Territorially marked by conspiratorial streets.

Sonnet from a Crow

I am the monarch of the palm tree
Meditator at the cemetery
Your twenty-four-hour watchman
Your super satellite disc.

I am your black coated advocate
The activist you can't placate
Your tireless campaigner for an
Environment at risk.

Al Gore is my missionary
Naomi Klein my visionary
India my prime example
Of re-cycling sense.

I'm your unpaid binman, your efficient foreman
With my invincible, indispensable, superman presence.

Monarch of the Bazaar
To Mario Relich

The coconut palm
Is my satellite perch
From where I navigate,
Plan and research.

The bazaar is my territory
Conveniently positioned
Directly under
My line of vision.

That house across
Has two top flats
Both with terraces
Open to flights

One has a lady
Who lays out square meals
Of fish bones and rice,
Bread and lentils.

Her neighbour is tight-fisted,
His shooing voice sore,
So I litter his terrace
With droppings galore.

And in the market
The potato man jests
Enthralled by his client's
Contours and zest.

I plunge like an arrow
And whoosh, I'm away
Secure with my prize
Before he can say 'hey!'

Let dogs cringe and beg
And cats hiss and haggle
With lost tails and ears –
They're beggars bedraggled.

While my feathers shine
With inky splendour
Untarnished by struggle
Or abject surrender.

Let chickens be plucked
And goats finely diced
I *shall* have my pick
And fly back in a trice

To my monarch's high tower
Alert every dawn
With my satellite power
Always switched on.

The Crow
To Joyce Gunn Cairns

Black-robed scavenger,
Fond of bare branches nearest the grey-clad sky,
Sitting on a slippery electric line,
A wretched spectacle, waiting to dry.

The world of colour bypassed your feathers
You were born –
A clumsy naked lump of flesh
In a flimsy unpretentious nest.
Not beautiful – nothing to boast of –
A hungry little shrivelled soul
Screeching with a voice not melodious,
For food –
Small specks of precious booty
That your sooty winged mother stole.

Your eggs were hatched along with the cuckoo's
Watched over with maternal care by a fastidious mother.
Fed, taught to fly by a species shunned by all.
At first it was a clumsy attempt –
Not an artistic smooth journey –
But a repeated beating of wings,
Breathless trying flights to the nearest window-sill –
Till one day, well-schooled in the art,
You left your uncomfortable abode,
Ready to befriend any bird, any man,
But always avoided, unwanted
Yet necessary for society to clear its
Discarded waste in bins and street piles
Before the clearing lorries' invasion –
Gliding through life as best you can.

Nobody wants you, adroit little thief –
Yet we do need you, astute little bird,
Leaving our garbage for you to clear
Between rubbish collection days,
Yet unflinchingly we shoo you away,
And compel you to trust to your wings,
And flee.

It is an endless search for the edible,
A continuous flight from
One human community to another –
A forlorn, watchful, resourceful being
Sensitive to the most unnoticeable lift of the little finger –
You flit away in a lightning flash
To find company with your own clan.

Thus you spend sunny days, rainy days, endless days
The herald of each new-born day –
A hoarse, broken reed alto,
A fascinating, swift, unostentatious crooner,
A grey-crested, black-robed, friendless scavenger.

The Sprightly Sparrow
To Debnarayan Bandyopadhyay

Can one analyse the frolicsome manoeuvre with which you
   flash by?
From branch to meadow
With your ever-changing shadow
To accompany you as you flit or float or fly?

The azure void above entrances you
The gay, tripping water enhances your cries –
The verdant green is dear, but dearer by far,
Is the telephone line, between the two worlds.

A peck at this petal, a glance to the right
A flurry as you scurry by –
The soft thud of berries, as you alight on a branch
And a commotion of rustling as you hurry by.

When a companion exasperates you
You never tire of speaking your mind
Wings flutter, feathers scatter in a noisy, aerial combat,
Shrieking and screeching and swinging around
Till a General Crow calls for order
And two guilty lieutenants hastily depart.

An unanticipated shower exasperates you
For it hurts your inherent dignity
To be seen in your ragged misery,
Dripping and helpless on a glistening lawn.

When deep in slumber, I am awakened by the sudden kiss
of a straw
And open my eyes to gaze at two bright, beady eyes
inspecting me below
Having lost your way amidst your spring task of
building your abode
– An untidy piece of workmanship for a sprightly,
charming bird!

Your seemingly carefree days
Are crowded with your active ways
To survive and thrive in your tiny phase
Of life that witnesses the lives of men
And women who trudge through pain
Suffer heat and wait for the rain –
Who never stop to look askance
At a playful speck of life,
Which seems beyond their care and strife,
A presence which traverses the sky, heralds the dawn,
Twitters incessantly, rocks the corn,
Whom footsteps astound and fireworks confound,
A loveable little symbol of caprice
Darting and flitting through life like a breeze.

Darkling I Listen
To Marion Geddes

It was in the stillness of midnight when the goslings
Had retired with mothers from their springtime dance
That my friend called me to step outside
While villages slept in the south of France.

Under the stars that lit a magnificent chapel
I could hear the deafening chorus of frogs, delirious
With song, who, my friend explained, were tiny denizens
Of the world with voices ambitiously searching the stars.

But these were not the vocalists
She wished me to hear. She told me to walk round
To the other side of her home, and there I heard
A heavenly choir that drowned the sound

Of the throaty clamour that had surprised me earlier.
'Listen to the nightingales' my friend urged
And I did, hearing the trilling and twitter,
The chirping and whistling, the harmony that surged

Through the branches above me. I was bewildered.
I asked, 'but which one is the nightingale?'
I could hear the smile in her voice as she said
'Only nightingales sing at night.' And in the pale

Starlight, a line I had carried with me
All my life was suddenly suffused with illumination.
Of course, Keats could not have heard the bird
Singing in full-throated ease seeking its twilight destination.

He heard it in the stillness of the night
And I heard a full choir, with a whole language
Of harmony, calling and answering,
Improvising in ecstasy with freedom and courage

That comes with the knowledge of dominance
And excellence as all other songsters slumber.
So I heard the nightingales singing
Their full repertoire just as Keats had done one summer.

The Eagle's Epic Journey
To Joyce Caplan

The eagle-keen gaze sweeps across the widening vistas
Like a cloud surveying its playground before rolling in.
Stereophonic vision, probing definition
That focuses on a fleck of an idea taking shape in the distance
A tale of spring-time hope, bobbing, bounding, unfolding –
The golden layered clusters of fish-scale feathers mirror the unfurling ecstasy
Of desire, which spreads its capacious wings, racing the cloud's fantasy
Its hooked beak a determined clasp
Like a seeking crane's targeting grasp
Now on a direct mission of deadly precision.
The intention soars, hovers and swoops – and in a trice
It scoops up in confident claws, a throbbing prize
Claimed by the king of skies
Challenging the supreme Creator
As it zooms swiftly to the zenith,
The sole deliberator
Shadowing the speeding earth
Assured of fame in an acquisitive game
Of mastery,
Holding its trophy
In a vicious embrace
With arrogant grace
Before it devours the life-beat,
Perched on the ramparts
Of its pinnacle, ready to sleep
With the deep satisfaction
Of a mission complete.

The Rock Climber's Vision
To Sukla and Ranjit Paul

The pickaxe aims one more time
In a tired effort to find a ledge-hold
The knuckles ache under pressure
The knees are keen to buckle under
As the boot scrapes up the sheer side
Grasping for a toe-rest while the other
Stands poised, waiting for the message to move on
Thoughts are crowded out as the concentration point
Focuses on the axe, the rope, the waist, the foot and hands
Crushing down the knowledge of searing pain
In grazed knees, blistered hands and bruised chest –
Suddenly like a vast tree disturbed, a whispering rustle
Lifts from the cliff crest and a shadow
Creeps over the landscape watching from
A bird's eye view, the lone trespasser in eagle territory
The anguish of goal-reaching is overcome
On encountering golden feathers cascading in multiple layers
Down a wary chest, the arrogant beak half open
The ochre eye alert, while the mighty wings
Flap in symphonic motion and then spread out
In the fullness of glory – a proud eagle's flight.

The Osprey's Observation
To Chrys Salt

And I have seen the wide White Nile
That fingers across global miles
The longest river that reached out
To see civilisation sprout.

As men came trading to its mouth
And rode its waves meandering south
Tracing its route with imperial dreams
Claiming the source of this generous stream

And I have flown these global miles
Following the ambition of the Nile
Borne along on powerful wings
I am the feathered king of kings

I've flown ornithological miles
Each year to the nourishing Nile
I've seen her in her fulsome days
Her mature beauty and reflective gaze

Her breasts were full with a mother's pride
She gathered millions to her side
Her waves could sway a continent
To settle down in deep content

But through the many thoughtless years
I've watched all caution disappear
As she was drained of her strength
Bit by bit with dark intent

She cries today with silent pain
Seeing vast stretches she can't drain
The drums are muffled, the music strained
As the Nile awaits reviving rain.

Crepuscular: The Urbanised Prowler
To Sara Wasson

Hush... this is the magic moment
When the Merchant City sleeps
As my father's raiment
Of wondrous wings sweep
Over stone tenements –
Scouring diurnal nests
Inspecting vacant lots
For a delectable feast
As his spring clutch awaits.

My mother awoke to life
In the scooped cove
Of a hoary oak
From where she learnt to roam
Till my father swooped
Down one night,
Won by the bonnie
Beauty of her flight
His queen of tawny owldom.

And I was born one spring
In the interstices of stone
The last sibling
Who has never felt alone.
And though I was the last
And the smallest
Of the nest
Five years ago
I knew I was best.

My parents were agitated
When one night they heard
That New Wynd would be lighted[1]
Against nocturnal birds
In a festival of radiance
That would keep the folk awake
Festooned with brilliance
Right up to daybreak.

How would the tawny race
Survive to soar and see
This torment they now faced
With nervous clarity.
But once the green fluorescent lights
Were zigzagged on our wall
I realised I was crepuscular as well
As being nocturnal
A special bird in flight
At dawn and twilight
And ready for the night.

So when the city is still and sleeps
I'm ready for my thrill and leaps!

---

[1] The Britannia Panopticon was a Music Hall in Trongate in Glasgow's Merchant City, built in 1857–58 on New Wynd when Glasgow was at the heyday of its imperial trade. The Panopticon was where Stan Laurel performed and it was one of the earliest buildings to be lit by electricity. It is now a listed building.

Night Watchers
To Rupsha

They were sitting as one community,
Each on its allocated perch
Still and silent as the night,
Whose denizens they were
Brought together now in a strange
Camaraderie which was not familiar to them
When they were free to scour the skies.
There they were – as if some taxidermist
Had frozen them in time for children
To stop and stare with awe, for adults
To linger with a sense of compassion –
Transient like the passers-by entering
The supermarket before dropping their pennies.

Many years ago I had seen a different scene
On a terrace where I had crept up to catch
The Hoogly's evening breeze as it revived
A hot, heaving city. It was the moment of Godhuli[1]
The cow returning home time of rosy dust haze
I knew I was not alone even before I saw them –
Not a community but a family of three, very like mine
Mother, Father and child sitting in a neat row
That the telegraph line allowed, not tethered as here,
But side by side and free, frozen for now while
The symphony of colour flowed in a swirling sea.
They couldn't see me, and I could touch them
If I wished, Lakshmi's[2] Owls, praying for the night.

---

1 The time when the cows return at sunset and the dust is raised from the ground.
2 Goddess of hearth, home and prosperity.

Serenading a Peahen

I saw your feathers droop and sigh
As the noontide sun bleached the sky
Which stretched languidly without a promise
To the horizon

Come glance at me.

If you care to lift your head and gaze
To penetrate the mystic haze
Your sensors will record a breeze
That gathers on the ocean

Come watch with me.

The vaporous mists have drifted free
And coalesced in camaraderie
Like floating ships that congregate
To a call for action

Come stand by me.

The storm clouds stream in dark display
They strain to churn the brooding day
The ocean wakes as thunder breaks
The sun has slipped away unseen

Come stay by me.

This is the monsoon's madness dance
They urge vast rivers to advance
The earth rolls back in ecstasy
Rocking to a lover's strain

Come sway with me.

See my quivering feathers lift
Delighted by this glamorous gift
As clouds swoop down to woo the sea
Which rings with their refrain

Come dance with me.

The Monsoons Break

A wild wind gathers over the bay
The nimbostratus screens the day
It streams across the seething spray
Glowering over expectant plains

The riverbanks have crumbled in
As sinewy streams have stumbled on
Through harsh cracked earth and panting fields
With wilting crops and tired yields

Till the welcome shadows come
Sweeping over praying homes
Thunder's drumbeats pulse and lift
The spirits of a land adrift

As lightnings flash with crashing might
And set the stage for new delights
The peacock's dance and peahen's glance
Conjoin to rock in joyful trance.

The rain comes crashing with intent
It coaxes parched lands to relent
It lights the sheen of tender green
While the peacock lives a lover's dream.

I Am Not Your National Bird Here: At Prestonfield House
To Rupsha

I watched from my perch
As you gasped with wonder
Spying me on the branch overhead
In my many-feathered splendour.

You warmed to me as your compatriot
And in your eyes I saw an affection
And more. Was it a tribute
To someone you held in high estimation?

Then you entered the great house
With purpose. I floated down
To join my mate. We browsed
Round plants and manicured lawns.

Ruminating on the door that would let you out,
And when you emerged, I sauntered
Across your path, a beacon of light
That you find irresistible. Your daughter

Swung towards my magnetic presence
You stood mesmerised, soaking in my fantail
Resplendent colours reminding you of the essence
Of a country where you have seen me dwell

In expansive generous spaces that forests open
In their depths or in sun-caressed growing fields –
Sampling berries or foraging grain
Overpowering reptiles those vast plains yield

But I have not been flown in from
The land where I belong. I have charmed
Travellers for centuries who were lured
By India's bounteous landmass and swarmed

Her ports and citadels where they discovered
My regal hues appropriate for the crown
Of the God of Love. My ancestors were lifted
To cruise across seas, the aristocratic gain

Protected and paraded as the badge
Of beauty and honour. Today I come –
A diasporic peacock in a packaged cage
Born and bred for generations on a farm

In West Lanarkshire, where I have not known
The joy of true freedom and choice
Of feasts once gathered at pomegranate dawns
Seeking leafy comfort when the sun paused

At its zenith. I was the forest's royal guard
Alerting its denizens to a lurking tiger.
I could scuttle swiftly across the ground
And soar above to rest when the vigour

Of the day was done, after my last
Gathering task was accomplished
And the sun's chariot hovered at dusk
Before its glow was diminished.

Here, your daughter waits for me
To lift my drooping thousand eyes
Into a fantail wonder. You will me
To quiver and soft step and sway in a daze

Of courtship abandon. But here there
Are no peahens for me to woo and win
I have no harem to watch over and care for
I am one of several males who do not dance and spin.

There are no monsoon clouds that glide
On a south wind's wings,
I am not their regal guide
A harbinger with glad tidings

Here I do not hear the malkosh[1] raag
That resounds across the plains
That have known summer's burning rigour
And prayed for welcome rains

So how can I dance here when I have never known
The rhythms of the seasons and a female's glance
I have learnt to brace the constant rain and chilling snow
But I long for the storms and love – the summons to dance.

---

[1] Malkosh is a late night raag, associated with the rains.

A Blackbird
To Alan Spence

He sings from the edge
Of rooftop rones, fluttering joy
On gardens warmed with hope

A banal street spins
To life, quivering to the
Strings of a blackbird's trills

The mother blackbird
Gathers crumbs for fledglings
Unperturbed by footsteps.

A Heron Sanctuary
To Dr Jim Jack

Beyond the loch
Lies a preservation patch
The chosen habitat
And designated sanctuary
Of long-legged herons.
This is sacred ground
Its swampy uncertainty
Defying the intrepid amongst
Swimmers and walkers.

It is a no-go swamp
For the prying birdwatcher
No voyeurism possible
As a host of ubiquitous
Swans, ducks and geese
Intervene, mucking about
In the busy loch

While beyond their ken
Are denizens of another world
Not dependent on charity crumbs
But poised for a protected
Existence.[1] They stalk
Across their catwalk

With the easy grace
Of supermodels
Who have no competitors –
Beauty queens in their domain

Assured of the applause
Of a world keen
To keep their magical world
Going as long as humanity lasts.

---

[1] 'The Grebe', which lies adjacent to Duddingston Loch in Edinburgh, is a sanctuary for the protected gray heron.

The Meeting Point: Mohona[1]
To Rachel Jury

Here by a reflective river
Reminiscing on a boat-building past
The turquoise hull of *Buena Vista*[2]
Stands still, its journeys over.
Here I am a heron taking flight
On a wing of fancy
Able to dream of a riverine terrain[3]
And conjure a mohona
Of meetings the boats once intended.

Here where discarded columns
And supportive concrete arms
Hold back bridges and roads
Letting echoes swirl around
Of traffic above and footsteps below,
I am a swan in a quartet
Waddling with my tribe
Across the empty road
To the weaving river

---

[1] A confluence of rivers, or the point where the river meets the sea. Here, it signifies Glasgow's link with the world in her boat-building days during the Empire through the migrations brought about by its globalised status then, and the continuing effects today.
[2] An old boat which has witnessed many voyages, now waiting to be scrapped.
[3] The Bay of Bengal, with its ever-changing waterways, at the mercy of the tide which brings the salt water in and submerges landscapes in moments.

To wade as dawn breaks,
Offering silent prayers
In ablutions I have seen
Performed by millions
In another mohona.[4]

Here where cars sneak in
To stay parked away from
The magpie eye of traffic wardens,
I emerge – the urbanised seagull
Uncertainly approaching the motorised
Milieu, hoping to find a break
In the flow, to rush across the road
My wings forgotten,
The 'WAIT' button – an unlearnt language,
A flown-in customer
From a mohona,
Waiting to embrace this generous space.

---

4 Through the centuries, thousands of devotees have stood waist-deep in water and ushered in the dawn every morning at Prayag or Allahabad, the confluence of the Ganga, Jamuna and the mythical river, Saraswati on the north Indian plains.

The Glasgow Thief

At a corner shop in Glasgow, a brazen
Thief with regular punctuality pilfered
A prized item every day without fail.
It was a particular flavour of crisps
That attracted the daylight robbery
Like an addiction that was unavoidable.

The guilty one had to be caught red-handed.
The CCTV camera acted with alacrity. It picked
Up the miscreant who came stealthily,
With halting hops, checking right and left
To avoid detection. It unsettled the prized
Packet gingerly from its neighbours and
Light stepped back to its waiting cronies
Guarding the pavement at the doorway.
The three musketeers, armed with their
Treat, retreated to the edge of the kerb
And expertly broke the seal to share
A feast fit for the princes of the air –
The chief robber seagull who was willing to
Savour his trophy with a pigeon and a crow.

Homecoming: In Search of Petrol in Loch Lomond Country
To Amrit Sen

After the humid haze of sticky Kolkata days
The sensible Scottish temperatures under slate grey skies
Brought with them the bugle call of the Highlands
Lifted from the depths of the lochs and distant islands.

The castle on the hill beckoned
Where Wallace's call for freedom
Echoed across fortress walls
Of a staunch defiant kingdom.

This is where the road meandered
Beyond motorways and service stations
Through dreaming Saturdays and
Laid-back mist-moored towns.

On this ecstatic road
Of abandon and romance
The dipping indicator
Arrested the driver's glance.

Then the quest began for the
Receding petrol station
Which could be closed, defunct
Or lost beyond the horizon.

The frantic call to the rescue team
The reassuring two hour wait
In the warm interior of a bakery,
Softening the desolate.

The van arrived, the coast was clear
We awaited the jerry can
But were told, health and safety held –
What we had was a pick-up van

With high-tech aids of levered ropes
And safety belts and wooden boards.
A remote urged our outsized car
To mount the deck offered.

And while we watched with unhidden awe
This meticulously engineered process,
The skies were filled with flutterings
Of migrants seeking solace

In a homecoming to the chosen trees
Where they had returned with the certainty
Of twilight rest amidst deep silence.
This host of starlings guaranteed us

A summer's deal that would heal
And restore the hope for the freedom
We sought on the road – to roam again
To loch and glen of Scots' historic kingdom.

A Valued Sentry: In Aberdeen

To Wan Ying and Malcom Hill

It is the official restaurant 'cat'
Who stands in sentry duty at the
Curtained beaded door of the spillage
Room of the kitchen, watchful for fragments
Of Manchurian chicken or Szechuan prawn
That wend their way to his dutiful stand,
A tribute for his pains, a package
He accepts with gracious alacrity.

The carpark is his reception area,
Every vehicle weaving in is noted
With a piercing gaze, then followed
And guided in, watched from the top
Of the neighbouring car, approved
In its parking space, and then
The sentry flies back to his old position
At the rear door of aromas,
The seagull cat on duty.

In Holyrood Park

The drive through Holyrood Park
Was unexpectedly halted as we braked
Behind the car in front. From the other
Side we noted a queue of interrupted
Drivers ruminating at their wheels, silent,
Patient – as the world waited with bated breath.
It was no accident that held up the
Rush hour concourse. So what was it?
The reason soon emerged like the sun
From behind a pregnant cloud, a freedom march
Of geese who had trekked laboriously from
The loch below in orderly file, a regiment
Goose-tripping to a silent victory band
Crossing the road at their imagined zebra
Point, their wings firmly folded, having earned
Their right to waddle walk in urbanised precision
While reverent humanity watched with awe.

At Hampstead Heath

To Christine and Daniel Barreto

Summer frolic unfolded round her
The plush green of a circus ring
For the cartwheeling pigtailed
Performer whose little brother gurgled in glee
As he leaned on his plump hands and pushed
His nappied bottom up in a make-believe somersault.

The beady-eyed warblers watched out
For hands holding plastic bags
Of bread crumb favours, while portly
Pigeons wove between ambling legs –
Gleaners with gleaming eyes,
Eager to win their trophies.

She spotted him cycling through the crowd
The serious, dreaming researcher.
He headed straight for the lake
And splashed over the shallow edge
Scattering the paddlers
With ducklings and cygnets

She rushed up to him and asked
In an accent he loved but couldn't locate
Whether he was all right. He noted
Her dimples, wiped his damp glasses
And suggested they meet and speak later
When he was dry and in a better position

On firm ground. And she agreed
As one does in London at Hampstead Heath
Where the world congregates
To pick crumbs and win trophies
And love takes wing on a summer evening
Celebrated by cartwheels and a baby's mirth.

Pages from the Memoirs of a Battery Hen
To Saptarshi Mallick

My first memory is of a crowded, smelly place
Where my mother was indistinguishable
From a harem of identical clacking women
With very little space to preen or relax.
We were a pretty competitive lot, scrabbling,
Squabbling for the food thrown at us without
Ceremony. As kids we spent time getting out
Of other people's way, afraid of being trampled
By many feet. There was no question of playing
Fun games or scampering out to see the world.

Every so often, enormous intruders came in
To pick up some of my mum's friends with intent
And we never saw their beady eyes again.
We had no dignity as we scuttled round
Eating, dressing, resting, shitting in that cramped
Space which was not much of a home.
I lost mum one day when I was busy sampling grain.
Then it was my turn one rosy morning, when I was a full-sized
Lass, to be spotted and dragged off, my screams
Making no impression on my hard-handed captor.

He passed me on to a young man who tied my
Legs and slung me with some of my pals to
Hang upside down like a bunch of bananas.
The world now was noisier than our room
As I saw it the wrong way round from the back
Of a bicycle, as we dangerously coursed through
Busy streets, competing for space between

Bullying buses and trucks, impatient cars
And tired rickshaws, each missing us by an inch
As we were bumped through the frightening maze.

We arrived finally where the ground stretched green
And the air felt deliriously free and playful. One by one
My mates were dislodged and disappeared. Finally
We stopped at a house with a garden that
Had more colour than the rooster that trumpeted the dawn.
I saw her soft sandals before I heard her mellifluous voice.
Her sari folds were as delicate as her hands that chose me.
The lad untied me from my mates and flung me by her,
'Gently,' she urged. He laughed and promised to be back
In an hour to dress me for her benefit. She unknotted the string.

My stiff legs felt life drifting back. She smiled and picked
Me up and took me through the veranda into a roomed
Space that was cool and calm like her very presence.
Her daughter was delighted to meet me and brought
Me some lentils which I picked at cautiously from
Her palm after many urgent whispers. As I ate, my little
Pecks were echoed by her. She said, 'kutush, kutush'.
And that became my name. I loved the clean, cement floor,
The refreshing fan waves. And soon I was exploring
All the rooms in this new place where I was the new star.

The father watched me with amazement and amusement.
He and the mother sat opposite each other at a table
Surrounded by books, where I sauntered in every so often
Cocking my head to check on each of them on either side
Which always made them smile. As the days went by, I settled
Into a pattern, no longer cramped by jostling crowds.
I roamed unhindered, admired by the daughter,

Lovingly caressed by the eyes of the mother. My food
Appeared like magic in a bowl that seemed replenished
Eternally and beside it was a bowl of sweet crystal water.

This was my paradise. Even their ginger cat, whom they called
Marshall Lalu, eyed me from a distance, knowing a princess
When he saw one. He slinked away unhappily, preferring
An outdoor meal as I watched him from the dining room window.
My favourite perch was the wash basin behind a yellow wall
Which I used as my own special toilet, which the mother
Kept meticulously clean after I had ruminated on it for hours.
One day the young man came back, with a silver sparkling blade
And told the mother he was ready to dress me that day,
Apologising for not coming back the day he had deposited me.

The mother said his services were not necessary any more.
Why he asked, had she done the job herself? I peeked at him
From behind her sari pleats and he gasped in disbelief.
She told him it was too late. Her daughter came out
And picked me up. 'Kutush is part of the family now',
She told him, as she stroked my orange crest. 'Even Marshall
Respects her, doesn't he?' she asked me. I crooned
In agreement and looked directly at his startled gaze
Confident in my newfound dignity that he could not
Take away from me, now and forever in my new kingdom.

What the Birds Say

When a seagull flies over your head,
you know the sea is near
When a woodpecker's rat-a-tat greets you,
the forest path is clear
When swallows gather in the sky,
you know that autumn's near
When a robin nestles by your door,
you know that winter's here.

When sparrows gather straw to build,
spring is on its way
When blackbirds sing at day's dawning,
it's a fresh spring day
When cuckoos call beyond your wall,
you feel the warmth of day
When magpies claim your lawn their own,
summer's come to stay!

The Owl and the Elephant
A tribute to Edward Lear and Vikram Seth

The owl and the elephant
Met by chance on a beautiful moonlit night
As the owl sat perched
And the elephant arched
His trunk to salute the sight.

This charming bird with luminous eyes
Melted his elephant's heart
He was mesmerised
His tail capsized
And his legs were like jelly on tart.

His trumpet squeaked with a tremulous beep
As he asked for the lady's hand
The elegant owl
Gave up her prowl
And joined the elephant's band.

They pranced through the forests of India
They sprinkled the water of springs
They serenaded the stars
With a hoot and guitar
Welcoming the sun each morning.

The leopard leapt away
The deer stood surprised
As they watched the elephant herd
With an owl spending years
Between an elephant's ears
Protected by monkeys and birds.

A Heavenly Concourse: In a Shattered Land

He looked up from the rubble
Of his home, chugging his red
Broken toy engine, and saw the tell-tale
Specks in the endless blue haze overhead.
His mother held his baby brother
Tight as she fed him, one hand
Lifted to shield the glare,
Her lips moving in silent prayer.

The cluster of specks glided closer
Looking for targets to drop
Their super-modern inventions to shatter
Whatever there was left to decimate
Around them and burn without concern.

And then his mother gasped with glee
His choked voice burst with ecstasy
As the deadly gliders were revealed
As travellers from far afield
A community of geese breezing with spring
Flying to breed, to feed, to sing
A symphony of life, of freedom on wings
A heavenly concourse of hope and splendour
A miracle of joy and wonder.

A Time to Leave

The time has come
For birds to forsake
This land
To abandon the
Nests they built
With dedication.
They will rise
Up with one accord
From trees that
Have cradled them
With deep affection and
The sun's benediction.
They will look out
For the Pole Star
For direction
And as the fires
Erupt in valleys
And on hills
Flaring through
Cities and claiming
The land
The birds will
Be a rainbow
Concourse, a cloud
Of hope, journeying
To a destination
Where love can
Return.

CATTERY
A CAT TRILOGY

*To Neil, the dedicated carer,
and Rupsha, who chose our cats.*

Mishti: Our Black Cat

Gambolling in a gyre of your own creation
Making swift dashes to retrieve your tail,
A gymnast – boneless, weightless, without trepidation,
Rippling into contours as you whirl or soar or sail

Across the room – an arrow released from tension,
A ballet dancer on points, pirouetting with delicate arms,
Jealously balancing a silly toy with the elation
Of an Olympic player, without any qualms

Of foul play, as your companion watches
Timidly, having been coaxed to abandon
His pastime, fearful of your scratches
Aware of your feline wiles, your guile, your wanton

Charm. You are here, then you are there
In the catch of a breath, a shooting star –
Erratic and copious. Slouching in rare
Moments of effortless boredom, you stare

Into space and lose yourself in self-gratifying
Dreams – unashamedly lazy, stretching and rolling
Into every conceivable, comfortable, satisfying
Angle – curling, lounging, lying, lolling...

We have melted in your soft, black sheen
Entrapped by the hypnotic glance of green intensity
That you cast on your mate and all who are keen
To be enslaved by your variable alertness and stupidity.

Toffee: Our Ginger Cat

You were obviously of the feral pedigree
Overwhelmed by the cruelty of humans
And the elements, driven to a corner
Where you would, if you could, build a hole
To be able to retire and disappear on a
Wish. Those traumatised luminous eyes remain
Imprinted in our memory, reminiscent of the degree

Of pain that you knew – an expression
We chose to change with time and a new
Experience. You were an addition to our
Resolve to let our attention revolve
Around one abandoned cat. Seeing you cower
And hiss in an attempt to dismiss us, drew
Forth a challenge that we took up against repression.

At the beginning you spent the daylight hours
Bulldozed – a carpet of soft quivering ginger
Sheltering under sofas and beds, creeping
In spells of quietness, between food and manger –
Two glowing embers, watchful and wary,
Counting the seconds for the outbreak of danger

Which broke like a pregnant cloud one afternoon
Scratching and tearing my flesh in self-preservation,
Defying the confines of a stifling cat basket cage
Which foreboded another terrifying trip for conservation
– A resilient table under a smooth, firm hand of a vet
Who had joined forces with ours to enforce your salvation.

Then the portentous cloud dissolved into tears
Of anguish. The claws curled and disappeared
Never to reappear. The ginger carpet swelled,
Rippled, recovered and reared,
The circles of flaming alertness melted into wonder,
Learning to trust and welcome what it had feared.

Noah: Our Felix Cat[1]

You were picked up on a slate-grey Edinburgh day
You were the last of a litter – unwanted
You flourished as soon as you came to stay
In a sprawling house where you sauntered

Through the rooms with a sense of ownership
That the two older cats had never mustered.
You were the cover boy your rescuer worshipped –
Handsome, debonair, confident, unflustered.

The older cats were curious and welcoming
You responded with snarling ferocity
Startling them to retreat from your unbecoming
Hauteur with their natural shyness and dignity

In the conservatory you were the jungle warrior
The glass panes reflecting your tiny delicate frame.
You saw yourself multiplied in every reflective barrier
Which you took as your adversary to tame

Into submission. So you hissed and turned
Your sweet furry ball of a body forever
Arched, your hair spiked, your tail a stiff wand
But you did not terrify, all your defences never

Achieved their target as your opponents
Adopted indifference and walked away
Uninterested and deflated, redolent
Of the days when they discovered that they

---

[1] Noah bears a striking resemblance to the black and white cat on the Felix cat food advertisement.

Did not have the speed and ease
Of the hunter in their middle age.
You then knew the sense of release
That comes when one leaves a cage.

Our daughter named you Noah, which at first
Caused a dilemma. You were confused,
Unable to understand 'No, No' – to your every burst
Of energy. Were you being greeted or dismissed?

You grew up to be the king of the neighbourhood
The night prowler, the day dozer
The swiftest hunter of every spring brood
Of birds and mice, never a loser.

Bringing unwanted trophies to the house
Which did not please your owners
To your amazement and surprise.
Bereft of the older cats you remain the gainer

Of sole attention, no longer a vision
Of fearsome intensity, but loving, warm and polite
The once tiny straggly, spikey demon
Transformed now into a purry delight.

The Unreachable Dream
To Ana-Maria Maguire

The cats watch dunnocks
And blackbirds
On the bird tray and on the
Grass. They twitch their ears
In alert signals and moan.
The glass window confirms
Their agony of tantalising
Nearness and unreachability.
When they do make up their minds
To dash through the house
Squeeze through the cat flap
And run under the gate
Into the garden, it is too late –
For the birds swish away
And the cats' springing leaps
Of super acrobatics
Come seconds after
Birds have taken to the
Skies or the hedge
At the edge of their dominion.
So the cats hunch back
Defeated, to crawl indoors,
And wonder how the birds
Are back to the bird table
Or the patio, when minutes
Ago, they had disappeared
From their horizon.

THE DISTANT AND THE NEAR

In Tiger Country

The great river in its seaward stage
Suddenly loses its singular identity
Branching out in sheer abandon
In myriad streams to form a complex network
Of waterways and inlets, sand strips
And landheads, islands and lagoons –
Mushrooming and melting with the tide
As it invades or retreats to the bay.
Sometimes these multiple rivers meet
And where their tears blend
Or where their freshness tastes sea salt
Is the Mohona[1] – the great dialogue
Of waters, the meeting point of diversity.

Here is where the mangroves grow
Those trees that whisper unceasingly –
Their convoluted roots and branches
An indistinguishable tangle, their leathery green leaves
Resilient to saline profusion and inland offerings
Bending, yielding, supplicating to the tide.
Their underwater existence is like a double
Image, a mirage of life murmuring and real.
As the tide comes without warning
And rivers change course, islands disappear
While others appear when the sea drifts away, spent.

And the mangroves switch back to prop up
The land they clutch at, the land where people
Lead uncertain lives, unable to anticipate
But willing to accept the rule of the tide.

---

[1] A confluence. Here, where the river meets the sea.

This is the land of the man-eating tiger,
Whose tracks are intractable with the tide changing
And fresh water mingling with salt at the Mohona.
It cannot set a blazing trail to rely on scent and memory
To retrace its soft-pawed catwalk.
It has learnt to swim with strength as the tide
Comes with sudden, sombre intent
Submerging the ground under its claws
As it feels the land shift and slip underwater.

This is where the beleaguered humans are easy prey
As they brave this territory of mirage
Of mangrove and monsoon, gathering honey,
Sowing crops they may not reap,
Rearing children the tide may keep,
Building dams that cannot resist the tide
In villages that are here for years and gone tomorrow
They fight an unwinnable battle.

What has turned this beast of the bay
In this borderland between salinity
And flowing streams to prey
On human inhabitants with alacrity,
Mauling the man of the swamps
In the territory of altering landscapes?
The beating drums to bewilder the beast
Who always attacks from behind,
Wearing masks at the back of the head
To deceive the wily cat, fail to avert his kill.
Makeshift scaffolds and flimsy fences
Give way to the dashing tide and leaping tiger
In the land of the Mohona where the Royal Bengal Tiger
Survives the ravaging tide that rules the Bay.

Inseparable: Wild Things[1]
To Lucinda and Paul Hare

In Kipling's Jungle they
Were predators, jealous
Of their territory, eyeing
Each other with caution
Ready to attack if challenged.
Sher Khan was the king
Baloo the fun loving, lifelong
Frolicsome bungling soul
And Leo just not there
As he stalked and prowled elsewhere.

They came to her playpen,
As two months old children
They cried and refused food
If separated. They played,
Loved and romped together

They grew up side by side
The law banned their captivity
So she took them to the wilderness –
To a sanctuary dedicated to the trio.

They showed that if allowed
To live together, creatures can love
And play together and become
Inseparable.

---

[1] This unlikely trio, a bear, a tiger and a lion, were rescued from a basement in Atlanta where they had been kept in cages. They spent a happier time in a sanctuary after being rescued, in adjacent enclosures, but could visit and play with each other and remained inseparable.

Born to Be Free
To Christine de Luca

I

I am a squirrel up your tree
You can climb up
But can't catch me
I'm frisky, bold,
Cheeky, wee.
I'll climb your shoulder
Grab your lunch
Scamper to the
Nearest branch
I'm in a hurry
My tail a flurry
Before you can say
'GOSH' and 'HEY!'
I'll scamper away
Up my tree –
Born to be free.

II

I am a fox
On your lawn
Frozen by the light
Turned on.
I come at night
To snoop around
Looking for some scattered bones
You might have left on the ground

For me.
You like my coat,
You like my sheen,
You find my gaze
Sharp and keen.
You keep your cats all locked in
I tumble over your full bin
You took my forests and my food
Your guns are aimed to spurt my blood
But when you open your back door
You'll find I've gone away once more
To the glen, across the meadow,
Born to be free.

III

I am a pigeon
In your square
I'm on your roof –
I'm everywhere
I roost on your ledge
I bask on your hedge
I'm courteous, discreet
I pick crumbs at your feet
You say you have a point
When you declare we are too many
But do I outnumber
Your human progeny?
If I litter your pavements
And mess up your tenements
Remember you took me from
The woods where I swarmed
And trained me to pass love letters on

You used me to scatter like leaves
On a breeze, your message of peace
I'm your symbol of love
In a soft winged dove.
I cannot fly far or flee
I have to scrounge in your city
Having lost the dignity
Of being born fully free.

The Hungry Ocean

The wind came hurling and unhindered
Willing to thrash me against the hard rock
Into an indelible fossil for future discovery.
As I held my ground stubbornly, I saw the sea sheet
Pricked by the raised standard of a solitary hand,
Then it was swallowed by the insidious depths,
The surface calmness a mockery of the demonic struggle
That had ensued to defeat its insouciant embrace.

The wind changed track, relishing its new role
As the sea's conspirator, willing to hurl
The bystander in me to join the lost swimmer
To feed the unmitigated appetite of a hungry ocean
Where I had watched a man drown helplessly and helpless.

The Storm

The storm clouds gather dark and hoary
The wind is howling through the glen
The hens are cooped in cramped tension
The sheep stay huddled in their pen
The cows stand still in anticipation
Waiting for the pouring rain.

And then it breaks with clapping thunder
Crashing barn and stable doors
Crackling lightening blinds the hill slopes
The horses snort and scrape the floor
The rivers rise with newfound fury
The sea invades the helpless shore.

Once old trees have been uprooted
Once tame horses have all fled
Once all villages lie stranded
Filled with water, silt and dread
Then the storm recedes in silence
Letting us pick out our dead.

The Sea which Sustains, Kills[1]

The ocean scooped
The fish lay bared
The water spouted
Children dared
The killer wave
Lifted its hood
And struck
Where children
Ran or stood
In swift, efficient
Mopping spree
It cleaned the shore
Thoroughly
While mothers watched
In agony
Scanning the receding sea
Waiting impatiently.

Fishermen in fragile boats
Lured to bring a bargain catch
Were never seen again afloat
With the killer wave's approach.

---

[1] The title is inspired by an article in the *New York Times* about the tsunami on Boxing Day 2004.

The sea is generous and free
It takes and gives handsomely –
Its arms were full when it returned
Strewing bodies it had drowned
Villages bereft of children
Streets of women without men
A rude awakening after Christmas
Along the fault-lines of earth's mass.

Let Me Be

In memory of Martin Luther King Jr and to Jackie Kay

Let me be your rambling brook
Rippling over angled rocks
Let me never flood your plains
To destroy life or smother crops.

Let me be your crystal dream
A waterfall that meets the stream
Let me meet my destiny
On rolling plains that welcome me.

Let me join the ocean's breast
Let me ride the surging crest
Let me see a confluence
That gives us sustenance

Where you and I can wander free
Create and live with dignity.

The Dry Season Ends
To Ian Brown

The sky's clarity brought
Days of unmitigated heat
As the trees stood panting
And the birds whistled with longing,
They brought missives
Of the monsoons elsewhere
And scoured the horizon
Sending bugle calls for succour.

It came last night without warning
Obliterating sunshine with intent
It blazed with the glory of fireworks
The splendour of explosive strength
Its volcanic roar sent shock waves
From the zenith to the earth's core
It opened the sluice gates of heaven's dams
Cascading over city and shore.

The steam haze has evaporated
The sky warns the sun to delay
A city recovers and fields are renewed
The birds play new melodies today.

The Bypassing Monsoons in June: From Kolkata
To Nigel Leask

The air was still and heavy with longing
Pregnant with the desire of sixteen million
Waiting for the water to break –
The deluge to come and invade the city.

The chariots of Arjun's army[1]
Had been gathering above the Indian Ocean
Waiting for the signal to gallop across
A panting nation, to rescue and restore.

The signal came late. The charge began –
The heavenly host-army descended
And rained its magical missiles across a peninsula
In multiple swoops, sweeping aside a fetid regime.

It had come every year, to change the tide
To displace and renew. But as the city watched
The skies, it skirted its hinterland, taking
A deliberate detour and marched to the hills.

The abandoned millions, bereft of succour
Remained where they were, at the mercy
Of a syndicate[2] that had rampaged
Over its green mantle at Jessore Road

Choked its reflecting waters at South City
Usurped paddy fields and fishing lakes
And cramped the skies with concrete
Stifled its life breath, willing Arjun's army to disdain it.

---
[1] See the battle of Kurukshetra as described in the *Mahabharata*
[2] A government-backed construction company.

Everest

To Kenny Munro

The tempestuous ocean dared to invade
The resisting land which folded in fury
Creating wooded prominences in a cabal which
Decreed to provide an impregnable army of
Incestuous mountains, conspiring to guard
The jewel in its midst – that vision of victory
Which has drawn swarms of ambitious dreamers to its
Sharp snow-laden ridges, its unclimbable crevasses,
Tired limbs reaching for its crest, aspiring minds eager
  to conquer
Everest, which stands cool and resistant to ownership,
Embracing three nations, its triangular base
Generously saluting each with sensuous acknowledgement
Of equal kinship – India, Tibet and Nepal
While the world pays homage to its Godlike gaze.

I belong to neither east nor west
Nor cold north nor deep south
I signify the ultimate rest
You long for in seeking truth.

On the Shore
To Alan Riach

Walking by the lonely shore
I thought I was alone
But as I took a bend I saw
A social picnic zone
With one whole crowd having fun
As some lay bathing in the sun
And others flipped across the ground
Frolicking and scuttling round
Making straight for the sea
Where they tumbled gleefully
Then sailed away gracefully
Watched by mates who lazily
Preferred the rocks to pass the day
As self-respecting otters may.

Seals and Shags at Plockton Firth

In the startling blue brightness of a northern sky
We saw them clearly, without binoculars
Our prow close enough to spy in sporting glee
But not invasively near to disturb
The lotus eaters' paradise of lounging loafers
Unapologetic in their sloppy, slothful abandon
Sunbathing their bulging shapes –
The mothers enjoying time away with pups
Who had none of the agility of
Baby flip flop curiosity, happy to lie
With inactive parent and watch
The occasional solitary swimmer without envy
Counting their blissful moments, while the males
Strayed away, gambolling in the open seas.
And beside this half-asleep indolence
We saw the vulture-like shapes
Of over-alert eagerness
Thin necks uplifted, pointed beaks
And small heads like periscopes
With antennae sensitive to every silver
Swish of aquatic life, pouncing with sharp
Aim – industrious, active and with purpose –
So different from the aimless, purpose-free
Existence of their 'other' race neighbours
With whom they colonised the rocks
With diverse yet unclashing missions.

The Rare Red Fox
To Sharon Gordon

As the festive sun slipped
Slyly behind the crest of Arthur's Seat
We raced its rays to our doorway –
But before we reached that familiar gate
A vision of racing ecstasy
Came bounding across a neighbour's wall
It skimmed like an ice skater
A gracefully choreographed
Olympian pole-vaulter
A ripple of musical muscle
In a dream-like heron's flight
A vision from a lost fairy tale
Its perfect body, its abundant tail
Leaping with lightning speed
Into our startled garden
Never alighting, never braking
A thing of beauty, truth and light.

Anxiety in the Glen
To Kathryn Simpson

In the shadow of the glen
Is the red fox's den
Where she waits for her mate to reappear.

Her cubs play in the light
Of the spring sun's delight
Tumbling over mother in her lair.

They do not sense the fear
That lurks beyond their lair
As their father strokes the bens beyond –

Foraging for food
For his little brood
To sustain their spirits and his bond.

The lochs are calm and pensive
The clouds are unresponsive
As the moment stands still for now.

If mother's mate comes back
There is promise of a pack
To kindle woods and quicken streams to flow.

The Galloping Vision: In Inverness-shire
To Clare Geddes

The sun had reached the end of its catwalk
About to retreat in glory and set
The applause was frozen in the shock
Of a sudden stunning silhouette

It stood frozen in haloed anticipation
Its hair ruffled like wisps of rain
Highlighted by the molten golden
Light that framed its neck and mane

The symphony then swept upon us
And heaven bent with renewed grace
The model orb spun out of focus
And on the earth an awesome race

Began, as the vision sprang to movement
Setting the captive rhythm free
From the limits of earth's raiment
Beyond the meeting point with sea.

From an amble to a canter
It set the beat which ruled the moon
And one by one the stars encountered
An amorous harmony that soon

Brought together slave and master
Locked in drum beats' breathless speed
As the earth skidded faster
Like a train from tracks now freed

Thudding through the feverish night
Sped on by the gathering hooves
Of lightning speed and heaving might
Igniting love fresh on the move –

On and on it raced unbridled
Round and round the field it tore
Till past and present moments mingled
As time unhinged its prison door

Letting the momentous vision
Challenge sea, sky and earth
Fragmenting the known horizon
In this fecund act of birth.

Migration

Stillness
Growth
Darkness
Hope

Tap tap
Knock
Crack crack
Shock!

Shattered shell –
I am born free,
Screeching siblings
Jostle with me.

The nest is warm
Tight and safe
My u-valley mouth
An expectant cave

My father's call
My mother's care
In flesh shred treats
Always there

A towering presence
Protecting wings
When blanketing night
Shrouds all things

The new-lit dawn
Startles me
Kindled colours
Flow wondrously

I feel my feathers
Strengthen and stretch
In perfect wings
That ruffle and itch.

Whooshing wind
On upturned face
Legs outstretched,
In a new-found race

I've kissed the wind
I've savoured meat
But the sun's revelation
Is the ultimate gift

My mother glides in
And urges me rise
In pecking order
We grope the skies

I'm awkward and clumsy
I flutter and yell
My mother swoops down
And blankets my fall

My small body heaves
With fear I haven't known
My siblings' chuckling cackle
Nearly puts me down

Till my father shouts
Come race me to that tree
I shoot ahead with vigour
And kiss the canopy.

I quite like this new perch
The leaves a glossy green
I watch my father fly away
I do not follow him

This is where I look around
And find a colony
Of birds like us in diverse nests
Living copiously

This is where I find my friends
Who, unlike my siblings,
Do not think I'm a big joke
Or a pitiful underling

I have found my new spring home
Where I will breed and feed
And seed this land for summer,
Giving up till autumn, my urge to roam
Anew.

Missives of Music

These rivers with their wilful whim have flowed through the centuries
Their waters replenished by the gifts poured in by tributaries
These families of trees in virgin acres and tended growth
Have sustained the lungs of this earth's vital breath
These icebergs have harnessed waves in their stoic frozen hold
Allowing floating freedom of continents where life unfolds

Great rivers are choked with industrial waste and urban filth
Their liberties are curtailed by super-dams diverting wealth
While forests are aflame, singed and swept aside for mines
An army of invisible wings fly out to devour humankind
The rains which forests sustain, recede as deserts expand
Fragments of icebergs once untethered makes the sea invade the land

But somewhere from the reverie of rivers sweeping to the sea
A boatman's haunting voice floats free in an uplifting bhatiali[1]
And from the depths of foliage where loggers do not rampage
The rhythms of tribal drums emerge with a message of courage.
At divergent icebound poles where polar bears and penguins roam
The arctic whales gambol with glee to a tidal symphony brought home
From oceans' depths and continents where all living creatures grope
Today for a fresh pledge to a future of commitment and hope.

---

[1] The bhatiali is the repertoire of boatman's songs composed and sung by them in the riverine area shared by Bangladesh and West Bengal in India.

The Distant and the Near

Open the door and let the green grass in
Stand by the loch and watch the wild swans spin
Greet the poppies at your door
Bless the seagulls as they soar
Let the oceans rise tempestuous, let the rivers brim.

Peep into your hedge and see the fledglings grow
Let your vision embrace hilltops clad in tranquil snow
Feed the fox that wanders free
Release the wasps to liberty
Return the bats to forests where no footsteps go.

EPILOGUE

A Message
To Neil

There is a deep thud that resonates
From the silence of the forest
A drum beat that reverberates
From the hilltop of hope
It weaves wistfully in whirling
Clouds of smoke from lonely
Cottages like samovars in fields
Pulsating with the vibration of life
Fluttering like a hundred doves in flight
Waiting to alight with the call of home.

Luath Press Limited

committed to publishing well written books worth reading

LUATH PRESS takes its name from Robert Burns, whose little collie Luath (*Gael.*, swift or nimble) tripped up Jean Armour at a wedding and gave him the chance to speak to the woman who was to be his wife and the abiding love of his life. Burns called one of the 'Twa Dogs' Luath after Cuchullin's hunting dog in Ossian's *Fingal*. Luath Press was established in 1981 in the heart of Burns country, and is now based a few steps up the road from Burns' first lodgings on Edinburgh's Royal Mile. Luath offers you distinctive writing with a hint of unexpected pleasures.

Most bookshops in the UK, the US, Canada, Australia, New Zealand and parts of Europe, either carry our books in stock or can order them for you. To order direct from us, please send a £sterling cheque, postal order, international money order or your credit card details (number, address of cardholder and expiry date) to us at the address below. Please add post and packing as follows: UK – £1.00 per delivery address; overseas surface mail – £2.50 per delivery address; overseas airmail – £3.50 for the first book to each delivery address, plus £1.00 for each additional book by airmail to the same address. If your order is a gift, we will happily enclose your card or message at no extra charge.

Luath Press Limited
543/2 Castlehill
The Royal Mile
Edinburgh EH1 2ND
Scotland
Telephone: 0131 225 4326 (24 hours)
Email: sales@luath.co.uk
Website: www.luath.co.uk